HOMECOMING
a quest for homefulness

by isabella motta

First published 2024

Text and illustration © Isabella Motta

The moral rights of the author have been asserted.

All rights reserved. No part of this book may be reproduced by any mechanical, photographic or electronic process, or in the form of a phonographic recording; nor may it be stored in a retrieval system, transmitted or otherwise be copied for public or private use, other than for 'fair use' as brief quotations embodied in articles and reviews, without prior written permission of the publisher and author.

The information given in this book should not be treated as a substitute for professional medical advice; always consult a medical practitioner. Any use of information in this book is at the reader's discretion and risk. Neither the author nor the publisher can be held responsible for any loss, claim or damage arising out of the use, or misuse, of the suggestions made, the failure to take medical advice or for any material on third party websites.

ISBN: 9789083444208

Published by Palaluga Books in collaboration with Forward Thinking Publishing.

FOREWORD

By Valeria Kechichian, Akashic Mentor - Energy Coach

We spend years, sometimes our whole lives, breaking ourselves to fit in into places we don't belong.

The quest for homefulness is one every being doing a human experience on Earth share.

Allowing the alien, stellar or just "weird" parts of you to arise requires courage. We were all raised in systems that pushes us to "kill" that part of ourselves, that connection to our essence.

HOMECOMING is Isabella's journey to feeling home in this human experience, acknowledging and uniting the human with the stellar. The visible with the invisible. Becoming one with her own Divinity.

We didn't come here to fit in. We came here to remember, to play, to grow, to be challenged and while doing so, inspire others to do the same.

Isabella has been doing that most of her life. Way before writing this book. HOMECOMING is a brave invitation to acknowledge all those parts of yourself that has been neglected or denied due to disbelief, insecurity, skepticism, fear or indoctrination.

In times when everyone wants to be a clone, we advocate for uniqueness.

It's an invitation to be yourself, no matter the kind of alien you are.

All colors, forms and shapes are welcome.

INTRODUCTION

By Isabella Motta

I wrote this book at 33, a year that felt symbolic in my own homecoming practice. More than writing it, it came pouring out, at first through textless watercolor paintings of this peculiar alien character that called to me from the depths of my soul, and then through words that echoed through soul whispers, dreams, meditations and playtime.

Playtime felt interesting during this period for me. My main passion for the last eight years had been longboard dancing, yet somehow, like many other of my known interests and hobbies, it had stopped making my body sing. I felt disoriented and full - too full - with stagnant energy that needed to come out.

One day, I felt an urge to try watercolor, and without thinking much about this seemingly random new interest, I walked out and bought the cheapest children's paint set I found close to my house. I didn't think much; I brought it home and painted the first page of this book. I'd recently started learning tarot after it came up in conversations with fellow classmates at my Jungian Coaching certification course and thought it might be fun to illustrate the readings I was doing for myself. Soon, this practice became a soothing habit I'd run to every day when I got home from work. It carried me through one of the most difficult and also most transformative periods of my life. *Arrival is as magic as it's disconcerting.*

Maybe because of my Asian roots and the cultural elements that shaped the impossibly high standards I held for myself ever since my school days, I'd always been proud to be a top performer in any activity I committed to. Undeniably, the flip side (or shadow) of that was a deep yearning for validation and the illusion that my value derived from productivity and how close I was able to get to perfection. I was coming off of what was likely one of the toughest years of my professional career, a year that made me question the foundations of the path I'd chosen.

Working with Diversity, Equity & Inclusion is as hard as it is rewarding. As a perfectionist over-achiever, mistakes or failures feel like a direct blow to the minoritized groups I work so passionately to defend. Compounded with my own identity markers as a lesbian woman and Brazilian-Taiwanese immigrant in Europe, it also felt like a direct blow to myself. And while it brings me hope to see Gen Z and younger generations starting to break free, as a millennial, I grew up embedded in hustle culture and chained to an adoration of the "girl boss narrative", placing on tall pedestals those who managed to juggle a demanding full time job with two side hustles, fitness, friendship, love, and traveling the world. Especially considering my identity markers, finding myself atop one of those pedestals gave me, for a brief moment, the feeling that I "made it". But as Maureen Murdock calls it in one of my favorite books *The Heroine's Journey*, that is but the "illusory boon of success". What follows is the "awakening to feelings of spiritual aridity" (which definitely feels as ominous as it sounds) and, finally, the equally feared and awaited "initiation and descent to the Goddess".

This book is the arrival at my descent. The starting point of this journey is at the gates of the underground jungles of my soul, at the very start of my own quest for homefulness. "Homefulness" might feel like an alien concept to those who are also immigrants, but to me, it's what has guided my quest so far, no matter where I physically found myself.

It takes a gentle type of courage to let everything crumble while embracing one's beautiful imperfections. These imperfections are actually markers of our shared humanity, of the miracle of being alive, inhabiting this body, on this planet. Home is not out there, somewhere between the job, the destinations we travel to, or the confinement of expensive walls we labor all our lives to acquire and die in. True home is within, is alive, and is calling for us to find it.

Maybe all this was supposed to happen.

to the peculiar alien character
that was hidden in the basement of
my soul - I missed you.

a special thanks to
my mermaid,
my sister, my mother
my father and my cats
Alice and Pretinho.

homefulness

[hōm-ful-ness] n.

───────────────

the practice of feeling
completely at home
in one's mind, body,
and soul, regardless of
physical location or
external circumstances.

before your story here starts
there's another story elsewhere
(and another, and another,
and another)

but the
journey
is far
and long

and what
happened
before gets
lost when
you awaken

arrival
is as magic
as it's
disconcerting

at first you approach
this world with
bright eyes and innocence

until they let
you know
there are rules
about one's
brightness

and they don't
love the
innocent

you quickly learn to shed
the alien parts that repel them
and making yourself small
becomes your best defense

you work and
you work and
you work

and eventually
it starts to
pay off

you get more than
what you wished
for you get things
you never dreamed
of before

one day you catch yourself
feeling homesick
for a home you've never
seen before

they say:
"how can
you feel
that?

compared to
others,
you've got
way more."

"that's true, I've got way more,"
you convince yourself and try to shake it off.

if only you listened
to your body,
who's telling you
loud and clear

your thoughts
and dreams are
endless lists
your mind is
pure pollution

your neck is stiff
your hair is thin
so you fill your house
with candles hoping to
clear the air

you're terrified
of losing
what you worked
so hard to get

you wish and pray for change
unaware that change
is already in motion

and then one day
you awaken
and walk out
into the unknown

you spend countless
sleepless nights THINKING,
"what did I do?"

until slowly
you put down
your burden
and wonder

why were you
carrying it
in the first
place?

what would happen
if you let it all burn?
if you turned upside down,
what would you learn?

you see,
if you
embark
on a
solo-journey
inwards

in search of
balance and truth

you may come to
find within you
everything
you will ever need

when was the last time
you allowed yourself
to lose yourself
in your passions
and then to find it
making magic
from within

when was the last time
you were reminded that
that magic is yours to keep?
you can't lose who is
already within you as
together you are one

when was the last time
you made time for
contemplation
of the magic weirdness
of the universe
of the magic
weirdness
within you?

the more you
question and
the more you unlearn
the further you
get in finding
who's buried underneath

celebrate who you found
and be warned:
this is not your
last happy ending

this is but the first part
of a slow and steady
initiation on creation
and manifesting

 the more you give

the more you get

 the more you grow

don't be impatient
to grow
rest doesn't need to be earned.
and if you don't rest,
you can't dream
and if you
can't dream,
you won't grow

rest is revolution
you can trust the universe
with your eyes closed

surrender. relax.
when you open your eyes
you'll see the universe
had always been there
manifesting love

the love you seek in others

you must first

find in yourself

once you find it
those who see it
they will love
your magic self

allow
yourself
to care

and be
cared for

smash all limiting beliefs
that tell you
you don't deserve it
you're not yet good enough
don't be naive
it's too good to be true

it will be true if
you believe it.
if you believe it
it will be true.

everything flows
when you become aware
of the abundance
of the universe

everything flows
when you become aware
that you create
your own reality

everything flows
when you become aware
that your intuition
already knows
the path forward

you learn
to create
to manifest
to alchemize

you learn to love
you learn to live
you love and live to learn

you learn to surrender
you learn to protect
you learn the only truth that matters:
you are the universe.
and the universe is you.

you see,
the work is not
about the job,
the house, the title
- it's about you.

so don't get distracted
by false battles
or dragged down
by false truths

remember,
in your world
the creator
is you.

you are free
to build a home
anywhere you go

you are free
to rest and
to sleep

you trust
that your body
knows

you are free
to dream your dreams
into existence
to enjoy life
to take it slow

now that you've regrown
the alien parts that
repelled some
protect those parts
fiercelessly so you
don't repel yourself

if you ever
get lost again
let your soul
flow through
your imagination

if you remember
you always have a choice
you will never
feel stuck again

remember to take a moment
every single day
to celebrate the home
you've built within you

and whenever
tough times
come again

(and they
will come
again)

see the world with
your gentle eyes
and remember the courage
that lives within you

everything
you were looking for
all your wishes
and dreams when you
first left home

were already within you
taking refuge in your soul

now you know
so don't forget
next time you leave
this world
you won't really
be leaving
you will be coming home.

HOMECOMING

a quest for homefulness

www.ingramcontent.com/pod-product-compliance
Lightning Source LLC
LaVergne TN
LVHW061531070526
838199LV00010B/455